Death of the Innocents

The story of drama and loss
caused by the fire at the school for deaf
children in Strabane in 1856

Clive Scoular

Published in 2013 by
Clive Scoular
Killyleagh
County Down

© Clive Scoular 2013

All rights reserved. No part of this publication may be reproduced, stored in a retrieval system, or transmitted, in any form, or by any means, electronic, mechanical, photocopying, recording or otherwise, without the prior permission of the publisher and copyright holder.

The editor gratefully acknowledges the help given unstintingly by his partner, Thomas Johnston, in the preparation of the layout and design of this book. Without his help the work could never have been completed.

ISBN 978-0-9574626-1-8

Also by the same author:
James Chichester-Clark, Prime Minister of Northern Ireland
In the Headlines — the Story of the Belfast Europa Hotel
Maeve de Markievicz, Daughter of Constance
John M. Andrews, Northern Ireland's Wartime Prime Minister
The Lives of Ten Influential Irishwomen
Six Famous Sons of Killyleagh
Eight Fearless Irishmen
William Craig: His Life in Politics

Introduction

This is a story that has to be told to ensure that six innocent deaf children who died tragically in the school fire in Strabane in 1856 are never forgotten.

Bob McCullough and I often talked about this terrible tragedy that happened all those years ago. We had discussed it with Derick Bingham, a local author and Bible teacher, and he had enthusiastically agreed with me to write a book on the life and times of Frances Alexander, the famous hymn writer.

The proceeds from Mrs Alexander's hymns and poems helped to build and maintain the School for Deaf Children in Strabane, which was established in 1846, and Derick would have been including this information in his book, as well as the impact the fire had on her and the local community at the time. Derick had started his research on the book and had planned to visit Strabane with me when he unfortunately became seriously ill. In a relatively short time he died from cancer before he could take the project any further. It has been my desire that the story be told and the efforts made by Derick be continued. To do this Derick's wife, Margaret, kindly gave me the book *Primate Alexander, Archbishop of Armagh* (1913). Derick had started his research with this book and had included a note in the book with the title he intended to use – *My Song in the Night*.

Bob, a highly respected representative of the Deaf community in Northern Ireland, has always championed the rights for a good education for deaf children and supported the need for this story to be told. I am delighted that he has taken on the task of writing the foreword to the book.

Christine Ward, from the Kinghan Church for Deaf People, has also invested a lot of time in helping with research for the book and has been an important link with the Deaf community in keeping the story of the fire alive.

I approached Irish historian and author, Clive Scoular, who had attended a Service of Remembrance at Kinghan Church for Deaf People in Belfast on 5 May 2013 for the six deaf children who died in the school fire. Clive had worked in a voluntary capacity at a school for deaf children in Glasgow before embarking on a highly successful social work career which saw him, as part of his overall responsibilities, overseeing the management of services for deaf people in Belfast. Clive took on the task of writing this book with enthusiasm and I know he enjoyed researching it. I am confident that it will secure a place for this tragic event in the history of the Deaf Community across Ireland.

Brian Symington MBE
former Chairman of the Ulster Institute for Deaf People
and Director of the Royal National Institute for Deaf People (NI)

Foreword

I read this book with mounting horror and anger. Some of the deaf children probably died from smoke inhalation even before the fire spread to their sleeping quarters and we can only imagine the terror and anguish they must have experienced behind locked doors and barred windows high above the ground.

Communication between the children and their teacher and caring staff was clearly at a very basic level and so the author, looking back so far in time, needed to determine what information was based on speculation or on actual facts. We read that the keys went missing and that there was even a suspicion of intoxication amongst the staff, although there was some controversy about this claim.

Did the children scream for help? Were they deaf from birth and probably unable to appreciate the importance of making loud noises to attract attention? Or were they just paralysed with fright?

There is a suggestion in the book that the blaze started from sparks left smouldering in an old besom, a broom made from twigs or branches. Are we to understand that the kitchen fire was left unattended or that the school was left overnight in the care of a person so befuddled with sleepiness or drink that he could not even find the keys of the children's bedrooms?

It is easy, of course, to be wise after the event. But for me the lesson is clear:

Deaf children. Locked doors. High windows. Poor communication. All add up to a deadly combination of fatal mistakes.

Bob McCullough
former columnist of 'Deaf Talkabout' in the *Belfast Telegraph*

Preface

When I was asked to write the story of the tragic fire at the School for Deaf Children in Strabane in 1856, I was happy to accept the challenge of bringing this forgotten episode in the lives of deaf people to the notice of today's population. Life for young deaf people in the mid nineteenth century was intolerable. At that time no one understood their needs, not even their parents; many people thought they were mentally handicapped and there were even those who considered them mad. I have researched the event to the best of my ability since it has been difficult to discover, not so much the actual events of that early May morning in 1856, but what actually happened to the surviving youngsters in the aftermath of the fire. Consequently I have used a certain amount of literary licence to shape the story using my knowledge as an Irish historian to paint a picture of what events could have been like in the mid nineteenth century.

I decided early on to concentrate on the fire and the influence of two very special women whose lives were, in many ways, dedicated to the needs of these children, Cecil Frances (Fanny) Alexander and Wilhelmina Tredennick. Many books have been written about the famous hymn writer but none, to date, about Wilhelmina, recognised as a founder of services for deaf people in the north of Ireland. And so this book revolves around these three subjects although reference is made to many of the other aspects which have already been covered in previous books.

My intention is clear. I want the reader to concentrate on the horrific events of the fire and its repercussions; I want the reader to appreciate the work done for deaf people by Fanny Alexander and Wilhelmina Tredennick and I want the reader to consider the steps taken since that day in 1856 in regard to the formation and improvement of the services provided for deaf people to this day.

There are many people I would like to thank for helping me in my task – Brian Symington, Christine Ward, Elizabeth McAughtry, Rachel and Henry Pollard, Hugh McGarrigle from Strabane and to the helpful staff at Londonderry City Library, at Omagh and Strabane Libraries and in the Belfast Newspaper Library. My partner, Thomas Johnston, has, as ever, skilfully prepared the book for publication and my friend, Joanne McCrum, has helped with some of the design work.

Clive Scoular
Killyleagh
November 2013

One

A shiny new pair of shoes

Ellen was excited. She was soon to start at a new school and one where her special needs would be well catered for. Ellen was deaf. She was eleven years old and, like all little girls of her age, she wanted everything to go well. Her parents were sad that they would be losing their lovely daughter but they appreciated that her education came first – and they had worked hard to find a place for her in this very special school. Ellen was gathering up and packing in her little suitcase all her clothes and shoes as well as her favourite toys. She knew she could not take them all but she was pleased that her mother and father were allowing her to take as many of them as she could. And not long before her departure, her mother had bought her a lovely new pair of shoes and Ellen was delighted with them. She would surely be warmly welcomed as a new pupil at the school especially with her lovely new footwear. For the first time in her life, although she was sorry to be leaving her parents, Ellen felt on top of the world.

It was Monday, 5 May 1856, as the little group of the Walker family set out for this exciting and very special educational establishment – the School for Deaf and Dumb Children in Strabane in county

Typical mid-19th century transport

Tyrone. Although they did not live so very far away from this bustling market town, it was going to be a first visit there for Ellen. They left their home early on that lovely spring day and set out for Strabane by horse and cart which, in those days, was the favoured mode of travel for those who could afford to do so. The lords and ladies of the vicinity may have had their fine carriages but Ellen was quite happy with her style of transport. When they arrived at the door of this lovely, solid looking two storeyed house, one which had only been opened just a few years before in 1851, they were greeted by the superintendent, Mr John Boyd and his wife. Ellen felt at home from the start because Mr Boyd was able to welcome her using gestures and signs. Although her parents and friends at home had always worked valiantly to communicate with her, it was only those who fully understood deaf people who could truly appreciate her needs.

Once all the necessary introductions had been made, Ellen was taken by some of the older girls to meet the other pupils and to be shown where she would sleep. The girls' dormitory was beautifully situated on the first floor and she soon found out that she would be the eleventh girl in the school. She was pleased to know that there were fewer boys in residence – just seven to be exact. Once she had unpacked her precious belongings, but still proudly wearing her bright and shiny new shoes, Ellen said a tearful goodbye to her parents. They were sorry to go but realised that this fine school was the perfect place for their daughter where she would continue to learn and be taught by people who fully understood her individual needs. For the rest of the day she played with her new friends and settled down. Later she met the head teacher in the school, Mr George Downing. It was strange, yet good, to be with young people who were deaf like herself, with the same educational needs. Her education to date had been limited to what her family and other people had taught her. Now she saw a bright new future opening up before her – her learning would soon start in earnest and she was full of the joys of spring.

However the vagaries of life were to unfold in a very different and cruel manner to what could have been expected for those young children in the school. Two mornings later, in the very early hours of Wednesday 7 May, Ellen found herself being driven from her dormitory by two elements – one human, her teachers, and the other, the dreadful sensation of heat and burning. The school, so new and holding so much promise for these budding scholars, was on fire. The inferno, horrible and heartrending, broke out very early in the morning. Ellen saw the teachers and other adults who had suddenly appeared at the dormitory windows encouraging her to get out – to come to the window or to run down the stairs.

But her beautiful shoes were her pride and joy and Ellen could not leave them because her parents would be very upset if she lost them. She had, in fact, escaped from the building but was so determined to retrieve her shoes even though Mary Anne Boyd attempted to prevent her from going back into the blazing school. So she crept back through the frightful heat, the dense smoke and scorching flames to try to find her shoes. But sadly she did not succeed in her endeavour and within half an hour she too had been consumed by the fire.

Ellen's remains were discovered later that morning by the adults who had come to try to rescue the pupils. For all had been in vain. Her shoes were literally the death of her. No one can tell if she would have been able to escape had she ignored her shoes, although there was always the hope that she might perhaps have been saved had she just got out, and stayed out, when first encouraged to do so. She would have been terribly scared and, even with the frantic gestures being made to her outside, she still went back for her precious shoes. In that appalling tragedy visited on these lovely, yet vulnerable children, six were to die, four boys and two girls, including Ellen Walker – the newest resident of just barely two days. The story of the fire will now be revealed but the loss of little Ellen in such harrowing circumstances epitomises the horrors of that night in that quiet country town of Strabane.

Two

The school for deaf children in Strabane

Before the events of this fire are described, we should take time to consider the whys and wherefores of this very special educational establishment in the pretty town of Strabane just across the river from county Donegal in the west of the Province of Ulster. The educational needs for most children in Ireland in the middle of the nineteenth century were at an early stage. There were schoolrooms throughout the country where children received their rudimentary learning.

However education for deaf children was reasonably well advanced. By the middle of the 19th century there were, in fact, seven establishments specialising in the teaching of deaf children throughout the island of Ireland. In Dublin they had the Claremont Institution, the Dorset Institution, St Mary's at Cabra and St Joseph's at Prospect. In Cork they had the Cork School for the Deaf and Dumb. On Belfast's Lisburn Road, there was the Ulster Institution for the Deaf, Dumb and Blind. Miss Gertrude Wright had also started to teach a few deaf children in Moneymore in county Londonderry in 1842.

Abercorn Square, Strabane (c1900) showing the memorial erected to Major John Humphreys

In the 1851 census report there is praise for the excellent services for deaf children. There were more establishments for the deaf in Ireland despite its smaller population and resources compared to the rest of the United Kingdom. There were well over 1,000 places available, with each of the children receiving in excess of five years education in the various schools.

In Strabane there was also a keen interest in deaf children's education. The good citizens of the area, aided and assisted by the local Anglican (Church of Ireland) clergymen, decided that there should now be a purpose built school to meet the needs of deaf children in their town. Its foundation stone was laid on 6 September 1850 at a place called 'Hazelwood', on the Derry Road (originally called Victoria Road) on the outskirts of Strabane on land obtained on lease from the Duke of Abercorn. By the summer of 1851 the school had opened with Mr George Downing, who was aged just 23, as head teacher and Mr John Boyd, who filled the position of superintendent. The school matron was Mrs Susan

Boyd, the wife of John. This new building, described as 'neat and commodious' and costing the princely sum of between £600 and £650 including furniture, provided a location for much needed education for those deaf children and from then on, until the tragedy of the fire, 48 children had passed through its doors. It was seen as a beacon of hope for the needs of young deaf children. The impetus for the school had been largely the brainchild of Major John Humphreys, a gentleman of some stature in the town and, with his clergy friends and the active support of the Bishop of the diocese of Derry, the school began to prosper and applications for admission to the school were coming in from all over the diocese and the neighbouring diocese of Raphoe, which mainly covered the county of Donegal. There were many events, such as fetes and open days, held over these years at the school and it became a real focal point in the town. The children loved having visits from the local townspeople with whom they interacted so well and were very popular with them. The people of Strabane felt honoured that their town had acquired such a prestigious establishment.

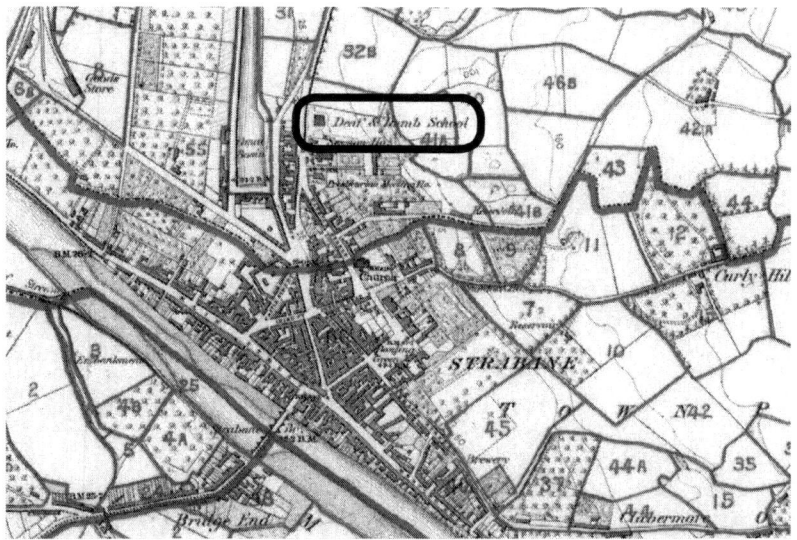

Strabane in the 1850s showing the location of the Deaf and Dumb School.

Three

The sting of premature death

There are some details concerning this disaster that are absolutely certain. Four boys and two girls died in the disastrous fire and their names are imprinted on the memories of those whom they loved and on those who care to understand and find out more about this lamentable event.

The boys were Andrew Patton from near Derry who was 11 years old; Daniel Doherty from Letterkenny who was 8 years old; John Brannon who was 12 years old and James Lafferty who was 15 years old. The girls were Ellen Devenny who was 12 years old and the aforementioned Ellen Walker who was 11 years old. As we pursue the story we come across the names of two of the boys and three of the girls who survived, but we do not know the names of the remaining seven children, one boy and six girls.

We know that this excellent and benevolent institution which was the school for deaf children in Strabane went on fire around 2am on Wednesday morning 7 May 1856 and was burned to the ground, the fire not being finally extinguished until 10 am. These are, so to speak, the absolute and incontrovertible facts. There are, however, the various versions as to what actually happened during the attempts to rescue the unfortunate children. All the local newspapers carried the story in their weekly editions – *The Londonderry Sentinel, The Londonderry Standard* and *The Londonderry Journal*, as well as the newspaper from the nearby town of Omagh, *The Tyrone Constitution*. During those years of the mid nineteenth century there was no published newspaper in Strabane itself. The journalists all took pains to cover the tragic events with a degree of professionalism although, in reading between the lines, they did come to some slightly differing conclusions concerning some of the aspects of the fire and its aftermath.

The fire almost certainly broke out in the kitchen on the ground floor of the school. The person who raised the alarm was a young deaf woman called Martha Elder whose room was directly above the kitchen and it was the smoke from the fire that wakened her and caused her quickly to go to Mr Downing's room to inform him of what was happening. Martha is described as 'Mr Downing's servant' and it is presumed that she was older than the other pupils and was perhaps around 20 years of age. It would seem likely, therefore, that she may have been a former pupil and had been retained by the school and apprenticed as a maidservant.

When Mr Downing, the head teacher, was thus aroused he immediately went to the kitchen but, finding the fire catching hold, took the precaution to close the door to prevent further air going into the room. The reports as to what caused the fire seem to revolve round the fact that a besom made of twigs had been used to sweep up the dying fire and that this little pile of material had caught alight and set fire to some wooden shelves which were close at hand. Another possible cause could have been some clothes drying on a clothes rack near the fireplace which went on fire. So there are two possible roots of the fire – the pile of swept up materials or the line of clothes. But, to be very fair to young Martha, she very quickly alerted those in charge and was available to assist with the evacuation of some of the children from their dormitories.

We then move to analyse how the staff members reacted to the critical situation. In the first instance it should be noted that the doors of both dormitories were locked, as it was the custom for Mr Boyd, the superintendent, to lock the doors at 9 pm every evening. Mr Downing,

Rev. George Downing
Head Teacher

having shut the kitchen door, was confronted by Mr Boyd who had arrived on the scene. And here the divergence in what actually happened comes to light. It was Mr Downing's contention that he asked Mr Boyd for the key to the boys' dormitory in order to open the door and allow the boys to escape. But he said that, for whatever reason, Mr Boyd did not give him the key. He readily admitted that Mr Boyd, in his confusion and agitation, may not have had the relevant key or for some reason did not give it to him. Mr Downing then decided on an action which, in hindsight, seemed a most unusual thing to do and might even have been described as reckless. Having vainly tried to smash down the door of the boys' room, he left the school premises and went down into the town, some considerable distance away, to try to procure a ladder as there presumably was not one at the school. This meant that one of the two senior men was out of the school at the most crucial time. It is reported that Mr Downing was absent for at least half an hour although he did find and return with a ladder as well as, at the same time, alerting the townspeople as to the horrific tragedy unfolding before their eyes.

Mr Boyd, in the meantime and presumably wondering where his colleague had got to, unlocked the girls' room and roused them, furiously signing to them to get out. Then he broke down the boys' door 'with the strength of a lion' and got them awakened. Whilst in the boys' room he encouraged two of them to throw some bedding out of the window although it appears that, rather then using this method of escape, the boys chose to run down the stairs. Mr Boyd then was able to throw another boy out of the window into the arms of the many concerned people who were waiting below. In his evidence at the inquest Constable McClelland confirmed that he was one of those people who had caught this boy. Head Constable Risk also stated that he had helped save six other children, three boys and three girls, who had also jumped from the window. Mr Boyd then threw himself out of the same window as he felt that he was beginning to suffocate and was caught in the arms of those same willing policemen and townspeople.

When Mr Downing eventually returned with his ladder, he propped it up against the windows and a volunteer ascended to see what could be done. By this time, however, the fire was raging out of control, and all that could be heard were the desperate cries of those children still in the room. Their fate by now was sealed and none of them survived. Some of them, almost unbelievably, on seeing policemen at the window and thinking something was wrong, dived under their beds never to survive. Some of the poor children even thought that there were robbers in the building and also resorted to hiding under their beds. Other local men then climbed up the ladder and succeeded in smashing down the heavy metal bars that were across the windows. But sadly and tragically their bravery came to naught, as it was impossible for anyone to enter the building for fear of their own lives.

It should be noted that there was some question as to Mr Boyd's sobriety at the time of the fire. It may or may not have had an influence upon the outcome of the tragic events. It seems that Mr Downing, when he first encountered Mr Boyd and asked him for the keys, considered that the superintendent had taken a drink. He was quick, however, to say that he still was very much in charge of all his faculties. Martha, too, said that she thought she smelt drink off Mr Boyd's breath. But, as in all such controversial incidents, there are contrary views. Unity Lafferty, one of the deaf children, when asked about Mr Boyd's ability to deal with this awful situation, declared emphatically that he was quite sober. More information about Mr Boyd's handling of the crisis will later be shown following both the inquest and the meeting held the next week to continue the investigation of the fire.

And so the dreadful horrors unfolded. The policemen and the citizens of Strabane who had arrived in double quick time were desperate to ensure the safety of the unfortunate children. They of course realised that the children were deaf and that normal shouts and calls would have no effect on them as it was obvious that they could not hear them. So they did the next best thing and ascended the ladder and gesticulated and signed to them to make their escape. Sadly most of their supreme efforts were to no avail. As we have seen some of the children were successfully encouraged to leap out of the window and thus some were saved in this way. Mr Boyd had himself also jumped and was caught by the crowd beneath. They did manage eventually to smash down the windows with their cast iron covers and subsequently the two prominent policemen, Head Constable Risk and Constable McClelland, arranged for a hole to be pushed through the dormitory floors from the floor beneath. They succeeded in doing this but, by this time, the remaining children were dead. Some of their bodies were so charred and burned that they were unrecognisable. For those who had to hand out their little bodies to those on the outside had tears in their eyes, never before having had such a sad and distasteful task to perform.

The memory of this gruesome episode was to remain with them for the rest of their lives. It was a most melancholy scene by 10 o'clock in the morning. This lovely building, which had given hope and much needed education to this group of deaf children, lay in ruins – a burning mass of timber and debris.

Four

The inquest

Within two hours of the fire, at 12 noon on that same fateful day, 7 May, an inquest into the fire was held in Strabane courthouse. To many this would seem to have been convened in almost indecent haste. Those who appeared as witnesses could hardly have had time to change their clothes or get something to eat and drink, far less have time to gather their thoughts as to how to respond to the searching questions which would be put to them so soon after the event. Nonetheless the local coroner, Dr Hamilton, summoned Major TWD Humphreys, the Reverend James Smith, the Church of Ireland rector, Sub Inspector Lynch of the police and Mr James Cochran, a prominent citizen of the town. A jury of thirteen townspeople, all men, was then selected to hear the evidence. The chief witnesses were Mr George Downing and Martha Elder, for whom Mr Downing acted as sign language interpreter. They repeated the story as already noted about the seat of the fire and the efforts to rouse the children. One significant witness, however, did not appear and that was Mr Boyd, the superintendent. It was said that he was not feeling well and was suffering from the ague (something like malarial fever) and was thus too delicate to be examined. In hindsight it would seem strange that this very important witness should not have been questioned at the same time as the other two main witnesses.

Later, in giving evidence, the Head Constable praised the efforts both of his men and of the local people who had turned up. Many other points of course were made. Why were the dormitories locked at night? Why did not more of the children make their escape down the staircase? And, above all, why was the town's small fire appliance so totally inadequate for, to all intents and purposes, it had turned out to be of no use whatsoever?

The coroner and jury listened intently to the evidence given. They appreciated the harrowing circumstances of the inferno which had only occurred that very morning. They may have wondered why Mr Boyd had not been produced as a witness at this crucial time; they would surely have felt ashamed and embarrassed that their own town's fire engine had been so useless although, on the other hand, they must have felt extremely proud that those who had come to assist in such awful circumstances had done a most worthy job. In the end they found that the cause of death was suffocation and that the building had been accidentally burned down. They did, however, express the opinion that the reason for locking up the dormitories should be looked into, inferring that there really was no reason for this and determining that it should no longer be the case. The police and citizens were commended for their swift and brave actions. It was a sad and despondent group which left the courthouse that afternoon. The journalists who had attended had much to ponder before they sat down to write their articles for the next editions of their weekly newspapers. It was a sombre scene, with tears in many eyes, that late afternoon on Wednesday 7 May 1856.

Five

The burial of the innocents

The very next day, at 4 o'clock in the afternoon, a solemn and muted crowd of people gathered at the parish churchyard in Patrick Street for the burial of the six unfortunate children. Their badly scorched and burned bodies, or what remained of them for only two of them had been positively identified, were placed in six coffins and carried to their place of interment. Those assembled were hushed as the rector, the Reverend James Smith, intoned the words of the funeral service as recited from the Church of Ireland Prayer Book. It was a moving sight with gloom and despondency pervading the gathering. The words of the service were almost drowned out by the wailing of many of those present, particularly those who were related to, or were friends of, the deceased. It was a short ceremony but yet another doleful memory etched upon the minds of all who attended.

As they left the graveyard the mourners passed by the ruins of the school, that once lovely and well-appointed place. They had many thoughts in their minds that day – how would the relatives of the children cope after such a tragedy and what would become of those who had survived. Would they be able to continue with their specialist education? Thankfully their prayers were answered as arrangements were being quickly made to relocate those who had survived. A local schoolhouse had been earmarked to receive the children which meant that they were able, quite quickly, to return to their studies.

It is hard to imagine, however, what was going through their minds. They had lost six of their classmates in horrendous circumstances and they wondered how they could carry on. Other locations, including the Claremont School for the Deaf in Dublin, had heard of the fire and had offered positions there if need be. The headmaster there had sent his heartfelt condolences to the teachers and surviving pupils. The establishment in Belfast was also available should help be needed. At this distance in time, it is impossible to track the survivors but at least we know that they were not abandoned. Amongst those who had survived were the little twin Diven sisters, Margaret and Anne, James Gallogley, John Middleton and Unity Lafferty all of whom had escaped the inferno by either running down the stairs or being thrown out of the dormitory window.

Six

The sorrow endures

On Tuesday 13 May, just six days after the fire, a further important investigation took place, again in the town courthouse. Although the people had had little time to mourn the deaths of the children, they realised the need to get to the bottom of any outstanding matters concerned with the disaster. And so it was that the governors and committee of the school representing the Derry and Raphoe Deaf and Dumb Institution assembled once more with Major Humphreys in the presiding chair. The governors were mainly Church of Ireland clergymen from different parts of the diocese – it being remembered that the school was under their care. There were in fact eleven clergymen, with the Archdeacon of Derry being the most senior cleric in attendance.

At the outset Major Humphreys informed the assembled gathering that alternative temporary accommodation had already been found for the surviving children in a nearby schoolhouse. This information, which some had already known about, was received with a certain amount of relief. The children, in their state of distress, were in loving and capable hands. This was important to know.

Thus it was that the Major explained the reason for this second meeting. He felt that not every aspect of the fire and its consequences had been well enough explained at the inquest which had been held the previous Wednesday immediately after the fire. He wanted as many people as possible to give their evidence. He really wanted witnesses to be under oath but respected those who did not want to do so and yet wanted to give further information. On this occasion, too, others of great importance to the events were to be examined, including Mr John Boyd, the superintendent, who had been unwell at the time of the inquest and had not shared his knowledge of the incident at that time. And, almost as importantly, all the surviving children were there although they were not required to give evidence under oath. It must have been an unbelievably traumatic time for them considering that they had lost their friends so tragically and, never to forget, that they were deaf and would need their answers interpreted for the benefit of the governors. But, even with these complications and difficulties, the witnesses were produced and gave their evidence.

To most people there, and especially to Major Humphreys, it was this first evidence given by Mr Boyd that concentrated their minds. There had, after all, been inferences that more could have been done to save the lives of the children and it was the case that stories were circulating in the town as to the possible culpability of Mr Boyd. He commenced his statement in rather flowery language. Major Humphreys, who had in past years served in the army with Mr Boyd, insisted that he got on with his explanations, which Mr Boyd then proceeded to do. He said that, on realising that there was a fire in the kitchen, he had shut the door to prevent further air getting in. This was already known and accepted. Then he declared that if water could have been brought to the seat of the fire, it could well have been extinguished. But he got no one to bring water nor did he do this himself. He then explained that he only had the kitchen keys and had to go upstairs for the keys to open the girls' dormitory. His meeting with Mr Downing was brief for, when he looked round, he heard that Downing had gone off into the town for a ladder. He went upstairs, got as many girls out of bed as he could and then smashed down the boys' door. He had encouraged a couple of the boys to throw bedding out of the window, which they did, but then he saw that they had escaped down the stairs and not out of the window onto the bedding. Finally he helped another boy escape by throwing him out of the window and following himself.

The policemen were then examined and Head Constable Risk, on seeing the fire engulfing the school, had enquired if the children had all got out for he had seen some of them running about the yard. However he soon realised that there still were youngsters in the building and, with some of his men, did his best to bring them out – sadly without success.

Martha Elder was again quizzed but this time she said she thought Mr Boyd was quite sober. Still others related their stories. William Kerr had gone with Mr Downing to get the ladder and, on return to the school, had been encouraged to get any children out that he could and forget about saving any of the furniture. Thomas Kelly and a man called Luke, who both worked at the Strabane foundry, as well as a Mr Jenkins, gave their accounts of seeing two dead bodies in the upstairs dormitory and that Mr Luke had had to hand out the badly charred remains of these unfortunate children to those waiting outside. George Buchanan and James Murphy, who worked as the petty sessions clerk, were examined and supported the contention that everyone had made every possible effort to save lives.

Then it came the turn of some of the surviving pupils to give their evidence. James Gallogley, for whom Mr Downing signed, had escaped down the staircase. He said that a boy called Doherty had also been very lucky. He had been afraid of the flames and had returned to his bedroom but had then been encouraged to make his escape through the window. Another boy, John Middleton, had also escaped through the window. Unity Lafferty, one of the girls, and possibly a sister of James who perished, confirmed that Mr Boyd was rousing the girls as best he could. She had escaped down the stairs and she told of the twin Diven sisters also being lucky enough to get out of the window. These little girls were examined too and they corroborated what had been said by Unity.

The daughter of the Boyds, six year old Mary Anne, was also able to tell the panel that, as they were getting out of the building, they had seen the unfortunate Ellen Walker go back into her room presumably to try to retrieve her precious new shoes. She repeated that she had tried to prevent Ellen going back into the burning building, but sadly to no avail.

The evidence thus concluded enabled the governors to agree that this had been a tragic episode and that blame could not be apportioned to anyone. Even in light of the original doubts about Mr Boyd's actions and indeed his sobriety, they found no one blameworthy. There had, however, been reports made in the *The Londonderry Journal* of 14 May commenting on well-founded local rumours that Mr Boyd, Mr Downing and the school porter had been on bad terms for some time. It would be fairly certain that Major Humphreys would have known of these stories but had deliberately avoided any direct reference to them during the enquiry. Perhaps he felt a little uneasy but, having considered the unhappy events, agreed to stick to his verdict.

The hearing had lasted for many hours. It had been a horrifying experience for everyone, especially for the deaf children themselves. The newspaper reporters were again in attendance all the day long and produced lengthy articles for their next editions. There was, it seems, through the Dublin paper, *The Dublin Evening Post*, a call for a government enquiry. Major Humphreys immediately confirmed that his team would be most willing to assist in such an enquiry but, after a number of weeks, nothing appeared to come of this rumour. In hindsight such an enquiry might have been welcome for it would have brought to more public scrutiny the arrangements and precautions that needed to be taken in schools for deaf children. The opportunity had been lost.

Seven

The town commissioners set up a fire committee

The following Friday, 16 May, the town commissioners held an emergency meeting realising that it was urgent to improve their own fire fighting measures. Clearly the existing appliance had been a disaster and that something needed to be done immediately. A fire committee of five Strabane men was quickly elected to ensure the provision of a much more efficient service to fight fires in the area. A new fire engine and more buckets, hoses and ladders were urgently required and they proceeded to order these necessary accoutrements. They procured ladders and hoses and sought tenders for the provision of a modern fire engine. They approached a firm in London to supply this essential piece of equipment but unfortunately there exists no record to confirm whether or not Strabane ever took possession of its new fire appliance. It seems, therefore, that another opportunity to improve facilities in the town and district had been lost.

Eight

What then did the future hold for the surviving children?

Alternative accommodation for the surviving children had quickly been found but a permanent arrangement was needed as soon as possible. The diocesan clergymen proceeded with great haste and a committee was set up to consider the various options available to rehouse the pupils and rebuild the school. They sought the agreement of the bishop for their plans to raise the necessary funds to build another school and he readily and confidently assented to their request. Around £600 seemed to be the amount needed for the restoration of the school for young deaf pupils of the diocese. Circulars were sent out to every parish requesting that a special collection be made in their churches on one of the Sundays in June. It was to be a calm but persuasive appeal and each of the clergymen showed their enthusiasm for the idea.

One of the first of these charity sermons was preached in Newtownlimavady parish church by the Reverend William Alexander, then rector of Fahan in Raphoe diocese but soon, in 1860, to be translated to Strabane, with its intriguing parish name of Camus-Juxta-Mourne. His wife, Fanny, had spent much of her childhood in Strabane and Major Humphreys was indeed her father. The proceeds from the sermon that evening were in excess of £15 which was a commendable start to the campaign. It was felt that this had been a good beginning and the hope was that it would not be long until the entire sum required would be gathered. A couple of weeks later the Reverend Alexander preached again, this time in Aghadowey church, and the collection amounted to over £17, including a generous donation of £5 from one of the gentlemen present. It is important to chronicle the series of these sermons for it clearly shows not only the honest intent of the clergymen of the diocese but also the real generosity of the people of the area. It was, of course, a time of great need in the district and was not long after the Great Famine which had decimated much of family life in Ireland, even in the Strabane and Londonderry districts. On 22 June £20 was raised after the Reverend George Smith preached at Glendermott church and it was noted in the press that several Presbyterians were in the congregation who also contributed to this handsome sum. Whilst much was made of the generosity of those in the Anglican congregations, it is certain too that members of all other faiths helped this worthy cause.

Camus-Juxta-Mourne parish church, Strabane

Nine

Awards to the police and townspeople

In some ways it may seem a little unusual to hear that, at the end of June, the Inspector General of the Constabulary Force in Ireland made awards to members of his force and to a number of the local people who had worked so strenuously during the fire to save the lives of the deaf children. He commended their brave actions, often without regard to their own safety, and sent a total of £21 to be distributed to the policemen who had helped. £10 was presented to Head Constable Risk, £4 to Constable McClelland and £1 each to the other policemen in the Strabane barracks. They were all sent chevrons to be worn on their uniforms which not only were tangible symbols of their bravery but which also earned them extra pension money when their time came to retire. The government forwarded £10 to be distributed to three of the local men who had been most active in the fruitless endeavour to extinguish the flames on that fearful night.

And so life was beginning to move on; the clergymen were preaching their charity sermons and the powers that be had acknowledged the heroism of so many.

Ten

The state of Ireland in the mid nineteenth century

For people in Strabane and in the immediate surrounding counties of Londonderry and Donegal, the events of the 7th of May 1856 were firmly imprinted on their minds. For there to have been a fire with such tragic loss of life was bad enough, but the tragedy was even keener given that the deaths were of six young deaf children who had succumbed in such untold horror. The memory would remain with them forever. But they were also living in a most troubled country in the middle of this nineteenth century. Ireland was going through one of the most difficult episodes in its history. The Great Famine had not long passed with the resultant loss of life and the inevitable emigration. The country's population at the beginning of the famine in 1845 was more than eight and a half million but by its end in 1850 over three million of its inhabitants had either died of disease and starvation or had sailed for the new world in north America, many sadly perishing on the journey.

That was the overall view but the question was – how did this catastrophe affect Strabane and its surrounding towns and villages? The answer is that it did not do well at all. Firstly the famine did affect the area quite badly. It is often thought that it was only areas like west Cork and Clare that were decimated. This is a fallacy for the famine hit almost every part of the island. At the time of the outbreak in 1845 Strabane had over 5,500 people but by the end this number had dropped to barely 5,000. The overall picture was one of destitution and deprivation with mothers and infants starving and the menfolk finding it impossible to get meaningful work. There was a great decline in the local domestic linen industry which had always provided a great amount of employment for the townspeople.

Another cruel fact was that, for many decades beforehand, the population throughout Ireland had become almost totally dependent on the potato. When the crop finally failed in 1847 the people of Strabane were desperate. Although the local landlords did what they could for their tenants there still were disputes amongst the local town dignitaries as to the best and most humane way to deal with the emergency. Many people died and many emigrated. The only possible chink in this cycle of distress was the knowledge that the local workhouse, opened as recently as 1841, would at least be able to cater for some of their needs – and so it did. In the story of the Irish famine the fact that 130 workhouses had been opened throughout Ireland just before the outbreak of the pestilence was nothing short of a miracle. Had they not been there the outcome would surely have been even more catastrophic. Strabane survived the famine – just.

And yet it was during the famine that the school for deaf children opened in its temporary premises in 1846; it was during the famine that the foundation stone for the school was laid in 1850 and it was just after the famine, in 1851, that the new school building was opened. The tragedy of the fire in May 1856 happened only five or so years after the end of the famine. The people were still suffering from its effects when this school fire was visited upon them. They were brave people as has been shown in their supreme efforts to save the lives of the children, but it should not be forgotten that, as a local and dwindling population, they themselves were still suffering from the repercussions of one of the worst calamities ever to be visited on any country.

And if we think that the famine was the only significant and tumultuous event that was present in the years around the time of the fire in Strabane, we should further examine the on-going tale of turmoil and trouble in Ireland. In the middle of the famine and just eight short years before the fire – in 1848 – there had been a rebellion in the country. The Young Irelanders, led by, amongst others, William Smith O'Brien, decided to rise against the government. It could be said that their efforts were only half-hearted and their only actual 'battle' was a skirmish at Ballingarry in county Tipperary known as 'The Battle of Widow McCormack's Cabbage Patch' when a small number of rebels took on 140 policemen. O'Brien was arrested, sentenced to death, had his sentence commuted, was transported to Tasmania, escaped to America and, at the end of his life, did return to his native land. In the very same edition of *The Londonderry Journal* of 14 May 1856, which carried that paper's first report of the school fire, there was also a leading article informing its readers that that very same William Smith O'Brien, who had risen against the elected government in 1848, had been given a pardon. In hindsight it seemed an unbelievable action for such men to have taken in the middle of the greatest famine ever to hit Ireland. But the point is that many earth-shattering events were taking place in the country at the very time when the citizens of the little county Tyrone town of Strabane were experiencing such a heartbreak of their own.

Eleven

How deaf people were treated in the mid nineteenth century

Life for people who were deaf in the 1850s and 1860s was difficult to say the least. However education for these members of society was reasonably good at that time with a number of excellent teaching establishments catering for them. The Claremont Institution in Dublin had been carrying on sterling work since 1816; the Ulster Institution (which also catered for blind pupils) had been serving the community since 1836 and the Strabane school had opened its doors in 1846. The three other institutions in Dublin and the one in Cork were also serving the deaf communities in their own areas. There were also, it should be said, a number of private individuals who saw the need to contribute to the education of these children like the previously mentioned school, under the tutelage of Miss Wright, running in Moneymore, not many miles from Strabane. And there was a tiny school for four or five pupils which was opened by Fanny and Annie Humphreys in the grounds of their home, Milltown House in Strabane. Fanny went on to become Mrs William Alexander - Mrs Cecil Frances Alexander, the famous hymn writer.

There had been a census of deaf children compiled by Sir William Wilde, the father of Oscar. He had accounted for nearly 500 children in Ulster who were in the five to fifteen years category who were deaf. From this figure it could clearly be seen that a large majority of those who needed the specialist education were not able to avail of it. Whilst the Strabane school had educated nearly 50 children since it had opened, this number barely scratched the surface of the challenge to educate all these children. The local diocesan committee, comprising all those Anglican clergymen, was perfectly aware of the difficulty and had been keen to increase the provision even before the fire at Strabane. This tragedy had, at a stroke, taken out much of the provision that had been available. They needed to rebuild the school – and quickly. That is why their support for charity sermons had been so high on their agenda for they needed a permanent solution for the survivors and all the others who required this specialist education. They knew how excellent was the education and training that their local children had already received – and it had to continue.

It has to be said that people at this time struggled to understand the needs of mutes as they were regularly and usually called. In general terms they were misunderstood. Even the clergymen on the committee, which worked on their behalf, took a stance that would seem alien to us today in the twenty first century. What follows is a quote made by the committee at the time of their initial fundraising efforts. 'Unless deaf mutes are educated at an early period of life, it appears that they are incapable of being instructed afterwards, a fact that shows the urgent need of imparting secular and religious knowledge to them at that season of life when alone they can receive it. Left to themselves, they become a burden to their relatives and friends, and frequently a cause of annoyance to the neighbourhood in which they reside, owing to their wayward and headstrong tempers. Their understanding is little better than a blank, and they are ignorant even of the existence of a God' (*The Londonderry Sentinel*, 23 May 1856). To today's reader this seems harsh and unloving, to say the least, but at the time it was the feeling and understanding of most people in society. The committee knew this to be the truth out there in 1856 so they had to do what they could to effect some change in perception as to the needs of deaf people. They were resolved to rectify the position and encouraged everyone to assist in 'providing for the temporal and eternal welfare of the poor deaf mutes who, if uneducated, would be without God in the world' (*ibid*). And it was also the case, sadly, that many people considered deaf people to be mentally unsound. Such were the misconceptions which prevailed in mid nineteenth century rural Ireland. Many mountains would need to be climbed before deaf people would find their rightful place in society but, at least, some positive steps were soon to be taken.

Twelve

The Cecil Frances Alexander connection

For a large part of the nineteenth century the name of Mrs CF Alexander was very well known. To many people her name became synonymous with the words of many popular children's hymns. Mention *Once in Royal David's City*, *All Things Bright and Beautiful* or *There is a Green Hill Far Away* and everyone knows the writer. As a child Cecil Frances Humphreys – known to her friends and family as Fanny – began to write verse. In her young childhood spent in rural and beautiful county Wicklow, Fanny just loved her surroundings; she also loved her church and these openings encouraged her to write. There were not many teenage girls writing poetry and verse in those days but it soon became known that this Fanny Humphreys was a special girl. She seemed to be able to express, in the most beautiful words, the world around her. She was living at a time when death came suddenly to even the most seemingly healthy children. And it mattered not if you were rich or poor, the scourge of TB, for example, simply struck you down and you were gone in double quick time. This actually happened to three sisters whom Fanny had befriended – within a few weeks they had all died of this dreadful disease. This drove

Mrs Cecil Frances Alexander

Fanny to write in order to express her deep sorrow and it was her way of consoling and being consoled.

Her father then moved from county Wicklow to county Tyrone in 1832 to work for the Marquis (later to be the Duke) of Abercorn. The family moved to Milltown House on the outskirts of the town of Strabane where the family of two boys and four girls soon settled down. Fanny, by this time fourteen years old, found it more difficult to make friends in this new place although she soon felt an affinity with the Anglican clergymen in the area. She spent her time writing more hymns and more poetry. The hymns that she wrote for children became well liked as they were simply worded and easily understood by even the youngest of children. They were descriptive and devoid of unnecessarily flowery and complicated language and ideal for youngsters to relate to the gospels which they were being taught in church and in Sunday School.

Her burgeoning interest in deaf people

Fanny and her sister, Annie, had met a few children whose lives seemed frustrated by being unable to hear or speak. These deaf boys and girls interested the two Humphreys sisters and they were determined to do something to improve the children's lot and enable them to take a more active part in society. This was a truly worthy view to take in an age not yet skilled or interested enough in understanding those who were deaf. They had a great friend in their rector, the Reverend James Smith, who encouraged them to approach their father and seek permission to set up a little school in a small building in the grounds of their home at Milltown House. The ploy worked and so was set up the forerunner to the school which was eventually opened in the town. At most there were just five children being given guidance and education. It may have been a low-key start but it was seen by many of the locals as a significant first step in acknowledging the needs of those who were deaf. The girls were commended for their work and one must never forget that they had to go to school themselves and so their care for their young deaf charges was something extra in their daily routine. It was clear, however, that they enjoyed what they were doing and had readily accepted their added responsibilities.

And so it was that, just a few weeks before she was married, Fanny Humphreys was present at the laying of the foundation stone, on 6 September 1850, for the new school for deaf children on the Derry Road which had the rather cumbersome title of 'The Derry and Raphoe Diocesan Institution for the Education of the Deaf and Dumb'. She could be proud that her own little school had been the precursor for education for deaf children in her part of the country. This new school would be another important teaching establishment for deaf children in Ireland. She had also sold some of her verses which she had published under the title of *Hymns for Little Children* and this made a significant impact to the total funds being accumulated for building the school but it also encouraged the local people to give generously as well. In October Fanny married William Alexander, whose career in the Church of Ireland was eventually to take him to the Bishop's house in Londonderry and, after Fanny's death, to the Primate's palace in Armagh.

This is one of the finest examples of Fanny's hymns from *Hymns for Little Children* which helped raise funds after the fire – and is still a popular hymn to this day.

The First Promise

Do no sinful action,
Speak no angry word;
Ye belong to Jesus,
Children of the Lord.

Christ is kind and gentle,
Christ is pure and true;
And His little children
Must be holy, too.

There's a wicked spirit
Watching round you still,
And he tries to tempt you
To all harm and ill.

But ye must not hear him,
Though 'tis hard for you
To resist the evil,
And the good to do.

For ye promised truly,
In your infant days,
To renounce him wholly,
And forsake his ways.

Ye are newborn Christians,
Ye must learn to fight
With the bad within you,
And to do the right.

Christ is your own Master,
He is good and true,
And His little children
Must be holy too.

Perhaps one of the most poignant verses ever written by Fanny Alexander came from this same little book and it epitomises her determination to bridge the gap between the hearing population and those living with deafness. It was by words like these that people began to understand and appreciate their needs – and to do something about it.

Oh, happiest, who, running o'er
With God's good gifts in mercy given,
Turn from their own abundant store
To teach the dumb the songs of Heaven.

The role of the rector's wife

After her marriage, Fanny moved to her husband's parish of Killeter near Castlederg in county Tyrone. For five more years the Alexanders remained there and Fanny spent much of her time helping those who needed her care and assistance. It mattered not a jot to Fanny to which congregation those who sought her aid came from and during her stay she become much loved by everyone in that area and parish. There is no mention in the archives of any deaf parishioners but it seems very likely that there would have been some who sought and certainly received her help. It seems that Mrs Alexander, the rector's wife, was the kind of person everyone could relate to – a truly Christian lady and a friend to all.

By 1855 William had been appointed rector of Fahan parish in county Donegal. By now the Alexanders had two children, Joc and Sprig (really Robert and Cecil John) and their third, a daughter Eleanor (Nell), was born in 1857.

It was whilst they were in Fahan that they were to hear of the tragic fire at the school for deaf children in Strabane. Having been so much involved with the setting up of the school and the detailed knowledge of the pupils there, Fanny was devastated, as was William. She mourned the loss of the six young children, a number of whom she would have known. What could she do now? She immediately set about writing a further little book of her poetry and sold it on behalf of the grieving families and the surviving children. Sales of the book, entitled *The Legend of the Golden Prayers*, which included not only her own work but also much of William's writings, too, went well and a considerable amount of money was collected. But the whole episode plunged Fanny into great despair which was only softened by her faith in God.

Here are a few verses from Fanny's poem *The Deaf and Dumb Child* written in the days of despondency following the fire.

The Deaf and Dumb Child

No voice nor sound for me had power
I walk'd as in a sun-lit night
The stillness of the midnight hour
Was round me all the noon-day bright.

I saw bright eyes on bright eyes bent,
The speaking glance I knew full well,
But the lips moved – and what they sent
To other lips I could not tell.

And tenfold more unblest than mine
His hopeless, heartless, thankless lot,
Who hears on earth no voice Divine,
Whose lip can speak, and praises not.

It is also well worth reading a poem of William Alexander's written at the same time.

Voices for the Dumb – Prelude

When her nest is scatter'd, a complaining
On the spray the little mother weaves,
From her heart's wild harp its sorrows raining,
Thick as shadows from the shaken leaves.

There are lands, wherein, when Death's white fingers
Tap at last upon the sick-room pane,
Send the neighbours all their sweetest singers –
Comes the minstrel of the cunning strain.

Sweetly are the singers measure keeping;
Sweetly, sweetly do the minstrels play;
Till the hot heart finds a vent in weeping,
As in rain the sultry summer day.

Nest and nestlings Death from us hath taken;
Ruin broods upon our labour now;
Ours is only like the music shaken
By the wild bird from the hawthorn bough.
Death climb'd up with crown of fire above him –
Not as sometimes to a child he comes,
Gentle, so that we can almost love him,
Knocking at the nurseries of our homes –

But with red eyes, mad in anger mortal,
And his red hair streaming wildly o'er.
Flashing fiery swords before the portal,
Hissing like a serpent at the door.

We are but as poor musicians, ringing
On their harps some natural rise and fall –
We are only like the singers, singing
At the children's lowly funeral.

Primate William Alexander

In 1860 the Alexanders moved back to Strabane where William had been appointed rector of that parish of Camus-Juxta-Mourne which means 'the bend next to the Mourne'. The present day church was dedicated in 1879 by William who had been appointed as Bishop of Derry and Raphoe by that time. The former church had been sited in nearby Patrick Street and had, from all accounts, rather fallen into poor repair. Fanny and Annie were particularly pleased that this fine new church had been dedicated to the Reverend James Smith who had given them such help and encouragement in teaching deaf children in those early years. It was somewhat of a homecoming for Fanny whose parents were still living at Milltown House and this meant that she could regularly visit her former home and keep contact with her aging mother and father. In fact John and Elizabeth Humphreys died within twenty-four hours of each other in June 1872 and Fanny and her brothers and sisters dedicated a fine east window in the new church to their memory which still adorns Christ Church to this day. It was during her time in Strabane that Fanny continued to write more and more poetry and hymns. Always in the back of her mind was the memory of that fateful day in May 1856 when the School for Deaf Children had burned and much of what she wrote reminded her of that terrible day. She was never to forget those children who had died so tragically.

Blue plaque at Strabane Academy, formerly Milltown House

The Alexanders spent seven rewarding years in Strabane. Their fourth and last child, Dot, was born not long after their arrival and during this time Fanny wrote more hymns and William continued to make his presence felt. They were a popular couple with everyone in the parish. William was soon being earmarked as a possible bishop and in 1867, at the young age of 43, he was elevated to the see of Derry as bishop there. The move to the bishop's house in the middle of the busy city meant all sorts of changes for the Alexanders. They left behind life in country parishes which they had enjoyed and where they had made many lasting contributions which improved life for those who lived in those rural parts. To move now to the city opened up new horizons for both Fanny and William. They made a conscious decision to separate their ways simply because William would be often away from the city at country confirmations and in Dublin and Fanny took the decision to stay at home and spend time with those who needed her help in that place.

As far as the needs of deaf people were concerned, Fanny kept up her interest and when she discovered any children who were deaf she did what she could for them. Back in Strabane her older sister, Eliza, who had remained unmarried, had taken a lively interest in the deaf people of the town and had become the secretary of the school for a number of years when it was in its temporary accommodation.

Corbels in St Anne's Cathedral, Belfast, depicting Fanny and William Alexander.

Thirteen

Was the school ever rebuilt?

The straightforward answer is that it was not. After so much effort to collect funds for the new school in the months and years after the fire, with charity sermons and the sale of Fanny Alexander's books and many other gifts and donations, the drive to rebuild simply appeared to have fizzled out. By 1871 the temporary premises were closed and the school officially stopped taking new pupils. Some say that the endeavours to raise funds were half-hearted and others, who had willingly contributed to the funds, lost interest. In the archives of Claremont School in Dublin, there is reference to the fact that five of the Strabane children were transferred to their care along with a payment of £130 although the exact date of this transfer is not known. There was also an endowment of £450 for two Derry and Raphoe children to be always maintained in Dublin so, at least, a small number of county Tyrone and county Donegal pupils would have been boarded and taught at Claremont. In later years a few children from the north west were admitted to the Ulster Institution on Belfast's Lisburn Road. But, to all intents and purposes, the schooling for the Strabane children ended there not so very long after the fire of 1856. The site at Hazelwood where the school had been remained empty for a long time although in the years just before the turn of the twentieth century the wealthy Gallagher family of Strabane did build a lovely house there. The Gallaghers owned at least one factory in the town, which gave employment to many hundreds of the local people, and they had decided to make use of Hazelwood for their new home. There is a story told, even to the present day, that there were two haunted rooms in the house where no one ever stayed because of the presence of the ghosts of the children who had died in the fire. Be this as it may but there are obviously still memories of that awful tragedy of 1856.

A beautiful little poem was written as recently as 2012 by Anne McCrea in a poetry collection compiled after a number of poetry workshops held in the Strabane district. It concerns Hazelwood and makes mention of the fire at the School for Deaf Children. This may be the first time in living memory that the children have been remembered and it will give, at long last, a opportunity for local people to enquire more into the tragedy that happened in their own town so many years ago.

Hazelwood

Epitaph
Grand and poor lived there
Children who could not hear or speak
Six children perished there,
Their end not mild or meek.

Espalier tress with thrush's nest
Wise arms stretched out, a language speaks,
Daffodil and iris colour the wet day,
Fruit trees, bark brushed with tar, one now
A lean-to after Hurricane Debbie
Came to town. I flit down corridors.

> *To my bedroom framed by a window with wooden bars,*
> *Cornucopia of fig and leaf edge*
> *The ceiling of the grandest room.*
> *Chimney stack, perching eagle on gable roof,*
> *Virginia creeper, hazel: the fairies' tree;*
> *Hazelwood, my childhood home.*

Anne McCrea

The education of deaf children from the Strabane area continues to this day but is more likely to be at a mainstream school with support from peripatetic teachers and classroom assistants. The memory of the fire had almost been erased from memory and, if people in the town are asked today what they know of that disastrous fire, only a very small number would have ever heard of it. There is now, at least, a permanent memorial to remind the people of Strabane in the form of a simple little gravestone, erected by Strabane District Council in 2003 in the Patrick Street graveyard, which lists the names of those lovely little children who perished that fateful May day so many years ago.

Fourteen

The life of Wilhelmina Treddenick, one of the greatest pioneers in the field

Wilhelmina Tredennick was born in November 1837, the year of Queen Victoria's accession to the throne. She was born into a fairly well to do family whose home was a lovely house called 'Fort William' not far from Ballyshannon in county Donegal. From an early age Wilhelmina enjoyed spending time with the local people who lived in her neighbourhood. Many of these folk lived in difficult circumstances and Wilhelmina soon found herself in situations where her help was needed. And she gladly gave it. She became very popular and felt a calling. It could even be said that she was indeed one of the first welfare workers to look after the interests of deaf people.

During her visits around the countryside she came across an elderly couple who lived in a modest cottage with their deaf son. It became obvious to Wilhelmina that the boy's parents were not able to cope. They felt totally detached from the lad and the atmosphere in the little cottage was strained. Soon Wilhelmina was calling regularly and getting to know the boy as best she could. But she too had problems so she went home and started to read all she could about the needs of deaf people. There was, however, very little for her to read so she took it upon herself to teach herself. She learned to communicate by using signs and, as time went on, the boy responded to her tentative, yet valiant, efforts.

She soon heard that there were, in fact, some services for deaf people in Strabane in the neighbouring county of Tyrone. The Derry and Raphoe Institute for the Deaf and Dumb had been established in 1846 and so Wilhelmina got to know those involved. She was just a young teenager herself at the time yet she took it upon herself to make herself known and to indicate that she would be very willing to help improve the lot of deaf people to whom she now dedicated her life.

When she was barely eighteen years of age she heard of the horrific fire at the school for deaf children in Strabane. She would have known the school and would have been a visitor there from time to time; she would have known most of the children there and would have spent time with them. She would have been devastated and, after doing all she could, she was confirmed in her determination to spend her life serving deaf people. She knew Fanny Alexander too and, although not in any way an intimate of hers, would have appreciated the work that the Fahan rector's wife had done before and after the fire when she and her husband were selling books of their poetry to assist in the rebuilding of the school.

For the remainder of her life Wilhelmina undertook sterling work. She assisted with and contributed to periodicals called *The Deaf and Dumb Magazine* and *Our Little Messenger*. She was a person who was determined in what she took on; she was a doer and not just a talker. In the years following the fire at Strabane she did what she could to help. But she was saddened when she realised that this wonderful school was not going to be rebuilt. She had hoped that the early surge of interest to start again would realise the dream that the school would rise like a phoenix from the ashes but she was to be disappointed as were so many others.

By 1873, which was seventeen years after the fire, Wilhelmina put her words into action and set up the Deaf and Dumb Christian Association in Belfast. She even took time out to go to the school for deaf children in Bristol where she learned signing and finger spelling from those who taught there. Some twelve years later, in 1885, the society was reorganised as the Missions to the Adult Deaf and Dumb of Ireland. Her will to act for those who were deaf in the north west of Ireland had become a reality. Those people could now go to Belfast and be integrated into society. Her concern also extended to young deaf women whose plight in an urban setting like Belfast was difficult and the mission hall she set up in 1888 at 7 Fisherwick Place (always affectionately known as 'FP') provided much needed residential accommodation and a social setting and here she acted as the first superintendent. At the outset the building was rented for £50 per annum which was paid by Wilhelmina herself and she even spent over £120 of her own money to furnish the premises.

Throughout her life she had great support from members of her own family. In fact two of her sisters were also interested in deaf people. One of them, Mrs Kingstone, who was the wife of the governor of Cork Jail, was keenly interested in some of the inmates who were deaf and she helped her sister to understand their difficulties. Another sister, Mrs Johnston, who lived in her native county of Donegal at Bundoran, also had a passion to assist deaf people.

Wilhelmina Treddenick died on 3 March 1891 at the early age of 53 at the home of her cousin, Lavens Ewart, at Ballysillan, Belfast. Her death hit the deaf community very hard for they knew that they had lost their most tireless and committed colleague and friend. Many even said that she had died so young on account of her total dedication and hard work. Her name is still remembered to this day as one of the most devoted pioneers in the field of deafness. In truth probably more needs to be done to keep her memory alive and it is never too late for this to happen. Perhaps today, in the early years of the twenty first century, this is the time to act. The Wilhelmina Treddenick Award was established in 2006, the centenary year of the Ulster Institute for Deaf People being located in the building at College Square North, known in more recent times as Wilton House. The Ulster Institute was formerly known as the Missions to the Adult Deaf and Dumb of Ireland, which Miss Treddenick had founded. Considering what she did for deaf people of her day, no stone should be left unturned to celebrate the work she undertook so selflessly. The words inscribed on her gravestone in Belfast's City Cemetery truly and fully epitomise the life of this great woman.

WT – friend of the deaf and dumb
Our friend she was faithful unto death
Day by day no day without a deed to crown it,
She went about doing good.

Wilhelmina Treddenick, 1837-1891

Fifteen

Services for deaf people in the years surrounding the 1856 fire at Strabane

Services did exist for deaf people in the years before the fire in 1856. The Claremont School in Dublin was providing excellent schooling and residential accommodation by 1819. The other schools in Dublin and the one in Cork continued to carry out their sterling service too. And in Belfast, as far back as 1831, attempts were also being made to help deaf children. Remarkably a young seventeen-year-old man, George Gordon, opened a schoolroom at the Congregational church in Donegall Street which gave a number of young deaf people their first opportunity of learning from those who were interested in them. Two years later, in 1833, the little school moved to King Street and even then some of the pupils came from outside the city area. The school fell on hard financial times but they soon received enthusiastic support, and the necessary funds, to continue their great work. Such was the clamour for places that further expansion became paramount and so a new site was found in College Street where the new establishment, The Ulster Institution for Deaf and Dumb and the Blind, was opened in 1836. Once again there was such a demand

*Ulster Institution for the Deaf and Dumb and the Blind
Designed by Charles Lanyon. Built in 1843 and demolished in 1963.*

for places that, by 1843, yet another building was needed. A move to Lisburn Road was then made to a fine new building, erected for the significant sum of £11,500 on the present site of the Medical Biology Centre of Queen's University.

And so it was that the needs of deaf people were provided in increasingly better and more efficient buildings. It was a credit to those, like Wilhelmina Treddenick and then John Kinghan and Francis Maginn, that the services for deaf people took such commendable leaps forward.

The Reverend John Kinghan became principal of the school on the Lisburn Road in Belfast in 1853 and also founded the Kinghan Mission for Deaf People in 1857 which has been at its present premises on Botanic Avenue since 1899.

Francis Maginn, who lost his hearing at the age of five, is recognised as the founder of the British Deaf and Dumb Association (now known as the British Deaf Association). He subsequently received an honorary degree from Gallaudet College in the United States of America and the officier de l'academie francais (officer of the French Academy) from the French government. He succeeded Miss Tredennick as superintendent of the Missions to the Adult Deaf and Dumb of Ireland (which, in 1961, became the Ulster Institute for the Deaf). He was responsible for setting up a Centre for Deaf People in College Square North, Belfast, in 1906, now known as Wilton House.

All three, Wilhelmina Tredennick, John Kinghan and Francis Maginn are buried in Belfast City Cemetery.

Ever present in the minds of those who were striving for excellence in the field were the plaintive cries of those six innocent children who perished in the school at Strabane in May 1856. No more fitting memorial than the ever-improving education for deaf people could possibly exist. And these services continued to improve as the years went on.

> IN MEMORY OF
> THE CHILDREN WHO DIED IN
> THE DIOCESAN DEAF AND DUMB
> INSTITUTION FIRE
> HAZELWOOD DERRY ROAD STRABANE
> ON MAY 7TH 1856
>
> JOHN BRANNON   AGED 12
> ELLEN DEVENNY   AGED 12
> DANIEL DOHERTY   AGED 8
> JAMES LAFFERTY   AGED 15
> ANDREW PATTON   AGED 11
> ELLEN WALKER   AGED 11

Let us never forget these six innocent children who tragically died in the fire.

Bibliography

Secondary Sources

Articles and Brochures

Centenary brochure – *Christ Church, Strabane, 1879-1979*.
Concordia magazine (Strabane Historical Society) 1995 (which includes the story of the fire).
Harron, Michael, *Fires and Fire Fighting in Strabane during the Eighteenth and Nineteenth Centuries* (which includes the story of the school fire).
Jackson, Peter and Maureen, in Deaf History Journal, Vol. 5, Issue 2 – *Britain's Worst Deaf School Tragedy*, 2001.

Books

Alexander, E (ed)., *Primate Alexander, Archbishop of Armagh*, London, 1913.
Bradley, J. et al, *The Fair River Valley – Strabane through the Ages*, Belfast, 2000.
Caul, Brian, *Francis Maginn – His Life and Times*, Belfast, 2006.
Hailes, Anne, *Turn on the Light, Mummy, I can't hear*, Belfast, 1989.
Hartley, Tom, *Written in Stone – the History of Belfast City Cemetery*, Belfast 2006.
Lovell, E.W., *A Green Hill Far Away – a Life of Mrs C.F. Alexander*, Londonderry, 1994.
McConnell, D., Symington, B., and Titterington, V, *Then and Now - an Intergenerational Project between Kinghan Church for Deaf People and Jordanstown School*, Belfast 2009.
Omagh District Council et al, *Shared Spaces*, 2012.
Pollard, Rachel, *The Avenue – a History of the Claremont Institution*, Dublin, 2006.
Symington, Brian & Carberry, John, *British and Irish Sign Languages – the Long Road to Recognition*, Belfast, 2006.
Wallace, Valerie, *Mrs Alexander 1818-1895, A Life of the Hymn Writer*, Dublin, 1995.

Newspapers and Publications

Belfast Newspaper Library
Belfast Newsletter
Londonderry Journal
Londonderry Sentinel
Londonderry Standard
Tyrone Constitution